Brighte
Grammar 1

An English Grammar with Exercises
New edition

C E Eckersley
Margaret Macaulay
Revised by D K Swan

Pearson Education Limited
Edinburgh Gate, Harlow,
Essex CM20 2JE, England

© Longman Group UK Limited 1952, 1987

First published 1952
This edition 1986
Eighteenth impression 1999

ISBN 0 – 582 – 55895 – 6

Set in 10/12 pt Linotron Times
Printed in Malaysia, ACM

Illustrated by David Mostyn and Jerry Collins

Contents

Each lesson is followed by exercises

Parts of speech: nouns

We use **words** when we speak or write a language. In English grammar we study the use of English words. We see how we change the words and how we arrange them to make **sentences** that other people understand.

We say that English words are of eight kinds. If we want to decide which kind a word is, we ask ourselves: 'What work does this word do in the sentence?' The answer tells us which 'box' the word comes from. These eight 'boxes' are the eight **parts of speech**.

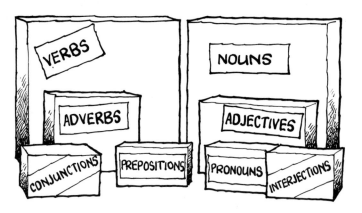

Let's look at the words from the biggest box: **nouns**. What work does a **noun** do in a sentence? It is a word that we use to name a person (*man*, *woman*, *John*), or people (*men*, *boys*, *Indians*), or an animal (*horse*, *dog*), or a thing (*house*, *town*), or an idea (*peace*, *size* etc.).

A noun is a word that names anything.

Exercises

A Write down words that name

six people	(*Example*: teacher)
six animals	(*Example*: horse)
six things	(*Example*: table)

You have written down eighteen words. What **part of speech** are your eighteen words?

B Pick out the **nouns** that name *people* in these sentences. There are 26 of them.

Example: Those women are teachers in my school.
Answer: women, teachers

1 The boy saw his brother.
2 The teacher speaks to his pupils.
3 My sister is a clever girl.
4 That boy is my friend.
5 There is a man and a woman in the picture.
6 Three doctors work in this hospital.
7 The children are staying with their uncle and aunt.
8 The man opened the door for his wife.
9 My father and mother have asked my cousin to come and stay at our house.
10 The soldiers marched through the town.
11 That little girl is my daughter.
12 The sailors were led by an officer.
13 A supermarket sells tea and sugar.
14 The chemist has a shop in that street.

C Pick out the **nouns** that name *things* in these sentences.

1 There is a pen on the desk.
2 The boy kicked the football through the goal.
3 Put the chalk on the table.
4 On the plate there were some apples and oranges.
5 The car went quickly along the road.
6 There were some new pencils in the box.
7 You can buy tea and sugar at the shop.
8 There are three windows in this room.
9 The bus is coming along the road.
10 The driver stops the bus at the corner.
11 The men are putting the boxes on the top of the bus.
12 The passengers are in their seats, and the bus starts.
13 Open your books and read the words on the first page.
14 There aren't any nuts on that tree.
15 The boy put too many nuts in his mouth.

D Pick out the **nouns** that name *animals* in these sentences. There are 21 of them. ('Animals' here include birds, fish and insects.)

 1 The dog is running in the field.
 2 Look! The cat has caught a mouse.
 3 I saw lions and tigers in the zoo.
 4 The bird is singing in the tree.
 5 Try to keep flies and other insects away from the food.
 6 Here is a hen with twelve chickens.
 7 We get milk from cows.
 8 There are horses and donkeys in the field.
 9 The eagle is a very big bird.
10 The kittens and the puppies were playing together.
11 A whale lives in the sea, but it isn't really a fish.
12 I am going now to feed the ducks and geese.

E Here are some **nouns** that name *ideas*. Use one to complete each sentence. We have completed number 1 for you.

journey time answer peace news noise price winter

1 What is the *answer* to this question?
2 In some countries, ＿＿ is a very cold season.
3 We measure ＿＿ in hours.
4 What's the ＿＿ of those shoes? – Forty dollars.
5 Everybody wants ＿＿ and not war.
6 Please don't make so much ＿＿. I'm trying to study.
7 Have you heard the ＿＿? The war has ended.
8 They arrived at the end of their long ＿＿.

F Pick out all the **nouns** in this story. There are 15 different **nouns** in it.

To cure a headache

A man went into a chemist's shop and said, 'I want something for a very bad headache.'

The chemist took a bottle from a shelf, held it under the man's nose and opened it. The smell was so strong that tears came into the man's eyes and ran down his cheeks.

'What did you do that for?' he said angrily, as soon as he could get back his breath.

'But that medicine has cured your headache, hasn't it?' said the chemist.

'You fool,' said the man. 'It's my wife that has the headache, not me!'

9

Lesson Two

Nouns: singular and plural

Look at these pictures.

Here there is only 1 boy, 1 girl, 1 dog.

In the next picture you can see more than one boy, more than one girl, and more than one dog. In fact there are three boys, four girls, and two dogs.

We know the words *boy*, *girl*, *dog* are **nouns**. Notice the little change in a noun when we mean 'more than one':

Singular	Plural
boy	boys
girl	girls
dog	dogs

What is the difference? Nouns that mean 'only one' are **singular**. Nouns that mean 'more than one' are **plural**.

With most of the nouns in English we make the plural by adding *s* to the singular.

11

Exercises

A Fill the space with the **plural noun**.

Example: One boy. Three ____.
Answer: Three boys.

  1 A horse. Two ____.
  2 One dog. Three ____.
  3 A car. Some ____.
  4 A big tree. Some big ____.
  5 One day. Seven ____.
  6 A shop. Some ____.
  7 The chemist. All the ____.
  8 A bottle. Several ____.
  9 An eye. Two ____.
10 One nose. A lot of ____.

B Fill the space with the **singular** form of the **noun**.

Example: Two boys. One ____.
Answer: One boy.

  1 Some houses. A ____.
  2 Some ideas. An ____.
  3 Nasty smells. A nasty ____.
  4 A lot of fools. One ____.
  5 Ten nouns. A ____.
  6 Ten spaces. One ____.
  7 Three animals. An ____.
  8 Two names. A ____.
  9 Things. A ____.
10 Five teachers. Only one ____.

C How do we generally make English **singular nouns** into **plural nouns**?

D Make two columns, singular and plural.

Singular	Plural
hen	chickens

Now write in the **singular** column, all the **nouns** in these sentences that mean 'only one', and write in the **plural** column the **nouns** that mean 'more than one'. We have filled in number 1 for you.

1 The hen has twelve chickens.
2 The chemist had a lot of bottles in his shop.
3 The boys are playing in the field.
4 My books are in my bag.
5 I have four fingers and one thumb on each hand.
6 There are pictures on the walls of this room.
7 The birds are singing in the trees.
8 The teacher gave us some lessons in grammar.
9 There is an apple on this plate.
10 How many windows are there in this room?
11 The referee blows his whistle and the players stop.

13

12 Open your books and read the sentences on page ten.
13 There are a lot of nuts on that tree.
14 The sparrow is a small bird.
15 Cats and dogs sometimes fight.
16 The elephant is a very big animal.
17 The man said his wife had a headache.
18 Tears came into his eyes.

E Complete the following sentences with **singular nouns**.

1 The ＿＿ kicked the ＿＿.
2 Give me your ＿＿.
3 I like this ＿＿.
4 My ＿＿ is on the ＿＿.
5 The ＿＿ writes on the ＿＿.
6 There is a ＿＿ on the ＿＿.
7 The ＿＿ is playing with the ＿＿.
8 I have a ＿＿ in my ＿＿.
9 He goes to the ＿＿ every ＿＿.
10 The ＿＿ is a very big ＿＿.

F Complete the following sentences with **plural nouns**.

1 The ＿＿ are playing with the ＿＿.
2 How many ＿＿ have you got?
3 There are three ＿＿ on the ＿＿.
4 ＿＿ are putting ＿＿ in the van.
5 The engine has six ＿＿.
6 There are ＿＿ and ＿＿ on the plate.
7 My brother has twelve ＿＿.
8 Open your ＿＿ and read the ＿＿ on page ten.
9 In the zoo I saw ＿＿ and ＿＿.
10 The ＿＿ are singing in the ＿＿.

Nouns: irregular plurals

For the **plural** of most **nouns** we add *s* to the singular. But there are some that make their **plural** differently.

1 Nouns that end in a 'hissing' sound (*-sh*, *-ch*, *-x*, *-z*) make their plurals by adding *-es*.

Singular	Plural	Singular	Plural
brush	brushes	inch	inches
box	boxes	fox	foxes
bus	buses	watch	watches
boss	bosses	church	churches

2 Some nouns that end in *-o* form their plurals by adding *-es*.

Singular	Plural	Singular	Plural
potato	potatoes	cargo	cargoes
hero	heroes	mosquito	mosquitoes

3 Nouns that end in *-f* or *-fe* generally change the ending to *-ves* for the plural.

Singular	Plural	Singular	Plural
leaf	leaves	wife	wives
half	halves	knife	knives
wolf	wolves	thief	thieves

4 Some nouns that end in -*y* change the -*y* into -*ies* for the plural. (Not nouns that end -*ay*, -*ey*, -*oy*. They add -*s*: *trays*, *donkeys*, *boys*.)

Singular	Plural	Singular	Plural
baby	babies	army	armies
lady	ladies	city	cities
fly	flies	body	bodies

5 A few nouns don't follow any of these rules. Here are the commonest of them.

Singular	Plural	Singular	Plural
man	men	tooth	teeth
woman	women	goose	geese
child	children	mouse	mice
foot	feet	sheep	sheep
ox	oxen	deer	deer

Exercises

A Write the **plural** forms of these **nouns**.

1 box, hero, potato, church, brush, fox, inch.
2 half, knife, leaf, baby, loaf, lady, donkey, fly, wolf, day, thief, army.
3 woman, child, tooth, man, deer, goose, sheep, foot.

B Write the **singular** forms of these **nouns**.

1 brushes, heroes, boxes, potatoes, churches, foxes, inches.
2 halves, wolves, leaves, armies, babies, flies, loaves, wives, ladies, thieves, knives, days.
3 sheep, feet, mice, men, deer, geese, children, women.

C What do we add for the **plural** to nouns that end in a 'hissing' sound? Give an example.

D How do some nouns that end in *-o* make the plural? Give an example.

E If nouns end in *-f* or *-fe*, how do they generally make the plural?

F Change the **nouns** in the following sentences from **singular** to **plural**. Notice that **plural nouns** do not have *a* or *an*.

Example: The farmer had a dog.
Answer: The farmers had dogs.

 1 The boy had a knife.
 2 The child came into the room.
 3 The man looked on the shelf.
 4 The lady gave a key to the girl.
 5 The cat caught the mouse.
 6 The leaf fell from the tree.
 7 The man and woman went to the cinema.
 8 The child saw a sheep in the field.
 9 The nurse carried a baby.
10 The boss had a new car.
11 The soldier got into a bus.
12 The donkey ran down the street.
13 A bird sang on the branch of a tree.
14 The foot of the deer crushed the flower.
15 The thief didn't see the policeman.

Lesson Three

G Change the **nouns** in the following sentences from **plural** to **singular**. Notice *a* or *an* with a **singular noun** when the plural does not have *the*.

Example: Soldiers stood outside the houses.
Answer: A soldier stood outside the house.

1 The nurses worked in hospitals.
2 The cats caught the mice.
3 The boys had knives.
4 The countries did not have armies.
5 The leaves fell from the trees.

6 The children rode on donkeys.
7 The men filled the glasses.
8 The boys had watches.
9 The policemen found the thieves.
10 We saw geese and foxes.
11 The oxen ate the grass.
12 The women told the children stories.
13 The thieves stole watches and radios.
14 The babies laughed at the children.
15 Wolves killed the sheep.

H Look again at the short story on page 9 and put all the **singular** nouns in one column and all the **plural** nouns in another column.

Lesson Four

Proper nouns

In Lesson 1 we had the words *boy, girl, dog, cat*. These words are **nouns** because they name people or animals. That is quite true; but most people (and some animals) have more than one name. The word *boy* means young male person – any young male person. Most boys also have their own names.

Let's look at a family. Mr and Mrs Brown (Henry and Susan) have three sons.

Henry Brown — Susan Brown

Jeremy   Richard   Mark

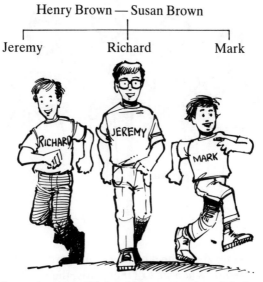

Jeremy Brown is a boy. Richard Brown is a boy. Mark Brown is a boy. They are three boys. The English word that names them is *boy*. It is a **common noun**. You can use the

English common noun *boy* for any young male person in the world.

The words *Jeremy* and *Richard* and *Mark* are **nouns** because they name people. But they are not **common nouns**: you can't use them to name any young male person. They are the special names of Mr and Mrs Brown's sons. In grammar we call these special names **proper nouns**.

Mr and Mrs Green (John William and Elizabeth) have four daughters.

John William Green — Elizabeth Green

| Grace | Karen | Pauline | Anne |

When we talk about the daughters, the word *daughters* is a **common noun**. When we call them girls, the word *girls* is a (plural) **common noun**. Their own names are *nouns* too – **proper nouns**. We spell these **proper nouns** with a capital letter: G, K, P, and A – *Grace, Karen, Pauline* and *Anne*.

Look at this map of England and Wales. On it there are
seven towns (or cities), four rivers, two ranges of hills and
three islands. The word *town* is common to all towns (that is,
it can be used of all of them). The word *river* is common to all
rivers, the word *island* is common to all islands.

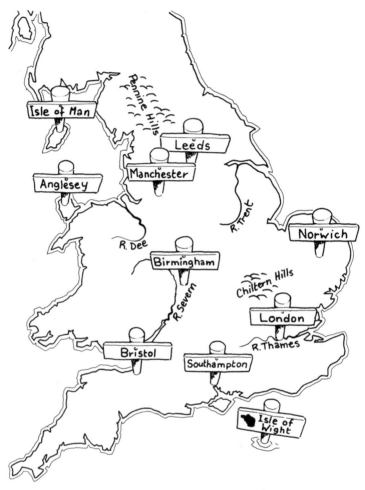

Now, here is the same map with the special names of these towns or cities, islands, rivers, etc. These names are **proper nouns** in grammar.

Nouns that are the names for all people or things or places of the same kind are called common nouns.

Nouns that are the special names of people or places or things are called proper nouns.

All proper nouns begin with a capital letter. The names of days of the week (Monday, Tuesday, Wednesday, etc.) and months of the year (January, February, etc.) are all **proper nouns**, and so should begin with capital letters.

Exercises

A Write down:

1 ten **common nouns** that are the names of things that you can see in your classroom (*Example*: blackboard).
2 ten for things used in games.
3 ten for things you can see in the town.
4 ten for things you can see in the country.
5 ten for things you can see in your home.

B Write down:

1 ten **proper nouns** that are the names of persons.
2 ten that are the names of places or things.

C Pick out the **proper nouns** in the following:

Example: Rome and Venice are cities in Italy.
Answer: Rome, Venice, Italy (not *cities* — it is a **common noun**.)

1 John came to our house on Friday.
2 Mary has a birthday in October.
3 The Nile is a big river.
4 Margaret has gone to Turkey.
5 London is the capital of England.
6 The *Queen Elizabeth* sails from Southampton to New York.

7 Kingston is in Jamaica.
8 The White House is in Washington.
9 The Red Sea is to the east of Egypt.
10 Our plane stopped at Bahrain Airport on its way to Singapore.

D Write out the following sentences with capital letters for **proper nouns** and the beginning of sentences.

1 harry lives in london.
2 lima is a very fine city.
3 my brother's name is george.
4 we flew to america on an air india plane.
5 the sudan lies to the south of egypt.
6 william shakespeare was one of england's greatest poets.
7 the nile is a longer river than the thames.
8 paris is the capital of france.
9 my birthday is on thursday, the 15th of may.
10 is delhi in pakistan or in india?

E Here is a short story. It has in it **common nouns** and **proper nouns**, but we have printed the proper nouns with a small letter. Draw a table and write the **common nouns** in one column, and the **proper nouns** (with capital letters) in another column. We have done the first sentence for you.

Common nouns	Proper nouns
sons	Tuesday, Henry Brown, Jeremy, Richard, Mark, London

A visit to London

Last tuesday henry brown took his sons jeremy, richard and mark to london. They live about fifty miles from london in a small town called greenfields. They went by train. It was an electric train with eight carriages.

'Here's a non-smoking carriage,' mr brown said. 'There are four seats over there.' He opened the carriage door, and they got in.

The train was a fast one. It didn't stop at knightstown, sandfield, pursley or didcombe. But it stopped at starwood new town. Some people got off there, and a porter put some bags of letters and parcels into the van. An old lady got into the carriage. She had a bag with her name and address on it: mrs m. smith, northwood street, croydon, surrey. Ten minutes later they came into waterloo station and very soon they were out in the busy streets.

'Come on, boys, we'll take a bus now.' They found a big red bus marked london bridge. 'That's the bus we want,' said mr brown and the boys hurried up the stairs and on to the top of the bus. As they went along, mr brown pointed out places and things for them to see. 'This is westminster bridge and there are the houses of parliament. We are crossing london's river now, the thames, and just over there is westminster abbey.'

'What's that monument on the bank of the river?' asked richard.

'That's cleopatra's needle. It came from egypt.'

'And what's that building in the distance with the golden cross on top?'

'That is st paul's cathedral,' said mr brown. 'It was built by the great architect sir christopher wren.'

'I want to see the tower of london,' said jeremy.

'We'll see that after lunch,' said his father.

'Where are we going for lunch?' asked mark. 'I didn't eat much breakfast, I was too excited.'

'We'll have lunch at a place I know in fleet street. Here it is, the cheshire cheese. We must get off the bus here.'

Nouns: possessive

It is possible to say, 'This is the book of the boy', or 'The dog of Mrs Smith was called Micky', or 'John is wearing the shirt of a man'. But English people don't usually say that. They say:

This is the *boy's* book.

Mrs Smith's dog was called Micky.

John is wearing a *man's* shirt.

This form is called the **possessive**, because it is used to show possession. It shows that something belongs to the person who is named by the noun – that the boy possesses the book, that Mrs Smith possesses the dog, that John's shirt is usually worn by a man.

The possessive form of singular nouns is made by putting an apostrophe *s* (*'s*) after the noun that stands for the possessor.

For ~~the cat of Mary~~ we write *Mary's cat*.

For ~~the house of Jack~~ we write *Jack's house*.

For ~~the foot of the girl~~ we write the *girl's foot*.

To make the possessive form of **plural nouns** there are two easy rules to remember:

1 **If the plural ends in *s* we just add an apostrophe**.
~~The house of the boys~~ = the *boys'* house.
~~The hats of the girls~~ = the *girls'* hats.

2 **If the plural does not end in *s* we add *'s***. There are only a few nouns whose plurals don't end in *s*. For example:

Plural	*Possessive*
men	men's
women	women's
children	children's

Examples: Their *children's* school is in the next village.
This store sells both *men's* and *women's* clothes.

The possessive		
Singular nouns	*Plural nouns ending in s*	*Plural nouns not ending in s*
These nouns take ⌐'s⌐	*These nouns take* ⌐'⌐ *only*	*These nouns take* ⌐'s⌐
lion uncle dog bird child John brother sister soldier son Mr Brown	babies soldiers sons girls uncles boys friends fathers cats dogs birds ladies	men women children

We use the **possessive** (*'s* or *s'*) form of **nouns** that name *people* and most *animals*. It is not generally used for **nouns** that name *things*.

So we say: the *teacher's* lesson; the *mother's* dress; the *dog's* foot; the *lion's* tail. But we say: the colour *of the book* (not ~~the book's colour~~); the roof *of the house* (not ~~the house's roof~~).

Exercises

A Write down the **possessive** form of the following. Then use it in a sentence.

Example: the teeth of the dog
Answer: the dog's teeth. He looked at the dog's teeth.

1 the hat of the man
2 the leg of the boy
3 the home of the girl
4 the stick of John
5 the wing of the bird
6 the voice of the child
7 the face of the baby
8 the laughter of the man
9 the shop of the chemist
10 the friend of my brother
11 the coat of Mr Huang
12 the tail of the cat

Lesson Five

B Write down the **possessive** form of the following. Then use it in a sentence.

Example: the teeth of the dogs
Answer: the dogs' teeth. The dogs' teeth were sharp.

1 the homes of the boys
2 the legs of the horses
3 the laughter of the girls
4 the wings of the birds
5 the voices of the pupils
6 the shouts of the men
7 the cries of the children
8 the shouts of the boys
9 the songs of the women
10 the friends of the ladies
11 the barks of the dogs
12 the friend of my brothers

C Make the following **plural**.

Example: the cat's eye
Answer: the cats' eyes

1 the boy's house
2 the girl's friend
3 the dog's bark
4 the man's shout
5 the lady's song
6 the woman's song
7 the child's game
8 the baby's smile
9 the bird's wing
10 the donkey's tail

D Make the following **singular**.

Example: the kings' palaces
Answer: the king's palace

1 the birds' wings
2 the children's games
3 the babies' smiles
4 the men's shouts
5 the boys' house
6 the dogs' barks
7 the girls' friend
8 the ladies' songs
9 the donkeys' tails
10 the women's songs

E Write out these sentences. Use the **possessive** form of the **noun** in brackets.

Example: My (brother) cat is in the garden.
Answer: My brother's cat is in the garden.

1 The man went to the (chemist) shop.
2 The name of Mrs (Smith) dog was Micky.
3 Have you seen (Wayne) new bicycle.
4 We heard the (men) shouts in the distance.
5 My (sister) friend is coming to tea.
6 Let us join in the (children) games.
7 That is a (woman) bicycle.
8 That building is the (Women) Institute.
9 Ellen is carrying a (lady) handbag.
10 Mary sings in the (ladies) choir.

F Write down the **possessive** form of all the words in the table on page 29 (*lion, babies, men*, etc.). Put each word in a sentence.

Example: birds
Answer: birds'. Look at all those birds' nests.

Adjectives

If I say to you,

A man came into the room

the noun *man* doesn't make a clear picture in your mind.

If I say,

A thin man came into the room

I limit the meaning of the noun *man*: you don't see in your mind a fat man or even a man of ordinary shape, only a thin man.

The word *thin* is an **adjective**. It tells us what kind of man we mean by our noun *man*.

We use an adjective with a noun to limit the meaning of the noun. The adjective qualifies the noun.

Here are some more examples:

a *thin* man	a *fat* man
an *old* book	a *new* book
a *heavy* box	a *light* box
a *good* egg	a *bad* egg

a *white* rabbit   a *black* rabbit

The words *man, book, box, egg, rabbit* are nouns. The words *fat, thin, old, new, heavy, light, good, bad, white, black* all tell us something about the meaning of these **nouns**. They tell us what kind of man, what kind of book, what kind of egg, etc. They are **adjectives.**

You will notice that in English the **adjective** usually goes *before* the **noun**.

a *red* flower
a *big* dog
a *long* journey

In later lessons you will see some exceptions.

Adjectives of the kind we have looked at in Lesson 6 (the words that tell us 'what kind') are **adjectives of quality**.

Exercises

A Put suitable **adjectives** before each of the following **nouns**.

Example: car
Answer: a red car

1 house	4 book	7 lion	10 headache
2 day	5 boy	8 train	11 flower
3 dinner	6 tree	9 river	12 dog

B Pick out the **adjectives** in the following sentences.

Example: Look at that old black car.
Answer: old, black

1 They live in a big red house.
2 Lloyd is a clever boy.
3 This plant has small yellow flowers.
4 Mr Chung is a kind man.
5 The camel is a very useful animal.
6 In New York they have warm weather in summer and cold weather in winter.
7 Mary has a new green jumper.
8 Lions are strong, fierce animals.
9 Cairo is a large, busy city.
10 These small apples have a sweet taste.

C Complete these sentences with **adjectives** from the box. We have filled in number 1 for you.

nasty cold new big sweet black favourite hot interesting small

1 The man bought a *new* car.
2 The teacher gave us an ____ lesson.
3 Henry has broken his ____ knife.
4 An elephant is a ____ animal, a mouse is a ____ one.
5 Do you like ____ apples?

6 In my country we have _____ weather in summer and _____ weather in winter.

7 Have you seen a _____ cow? We have lost it.

8 Mr Brown is not a _____ man.

D Read this short story. Then make 2 columns with the headings **adjectives** and **nouns**. In the first column write down each **adjective** you find in the story. In the second column write the **noun** that the **adjective** goes with. We have printed the **adjectives** and **nouns** from the first sentence for you as an example.

Adjectives	Nouns
poor	woodcutter
big	piece
wide	river

The woodcutter and the fairy

A poor woodcutter was cutting a big piece of wood near a wide river. Suddenly his old axe slipped from his hand and fell into the deep water. He was a sad man because he had lost his only axe. But suddenly a lovely, bright fairy appeared.

'What's the matter?' she asked the unhappy woodcutter.

35

'I have lost my old axe,' he said. 'It fell into the deep water.'

The fairy showed him a gold axe and said, 'Is this yours?'

'No,' said the woodcutter.

The fairy then showed him a silver axe and said again in her clear voice, 'Is this yours?'

'No,' answered the woodcutter.

Then she showed him a common, iron axe with an old, wooden handle.

'Yes, that's mine,' said the happy woodcutter.

'I know,' said the kind fairy. 'I only wanted a true answer. You are an honest man, so I can give you the gold axe and the silver axe as well as the old iron axe.'

Adjectives of quantity

There are several other kinds of adjectives besides adjectives of quality. There are, for example, adjectives that tell you 'how much' or 'how many'.

I have *two* eyes.

There are *twenty* books on the desk.

These are called **adjectives of quantity**.

Here is a little song with some **adjectives of quantity** in it.

Ten green bottles

There were ten green bottles standing on the wall,
Ten green bottles standing on the wall,
And if one green bottle should accidentally fall,
There'd be nine green bottles standing on the wall.

After this verse you continue:
There were nine green bottles standing on the wall,
Nine green bottles standing on the wall,
And if one green bottle should accidentally fall,
There'd be eight green bottles standing on the wall.

Then, 'There were eight . . .' and so on, until you come to:

'There was one green bottle . . .' and the last line will be 'There'd be no green bottles standing on the wall.' And the word *no* here is also an **adjective of quantity**.

Much and *many* are also **adjectives of quantity**. They tell us the quantity but not so definitely as the numbers *one, two, three* etc.

Much is used with **singular nouns**; *many* with **plural nouns** and we almost always use them with *not* or *n't*.

I do*n't* have *many* friends in Cairo.

We did*n't* have *much* rain this morning.

There are *not many* apples on that tree.

I did*n't* eat *much* breakfast this morning.

Adjectives of quantity show 'how much' or 'how many'.

Exercise

Complete the sentences with an **adjective of quantity** in each of the blank spaces.

1 There were ＿＿ bottles on the wall.
2 In the last verse of the song there were ＿＿ bottles on the wall.
3 There are not ＿＿ pictures in that book.
4 I have ＿＿ eyes and ＿＿ nose.
5 We hadn't ＿＿ time to do our work.
6 Ali didn't spend ＿＿ money on his holiday.
7 There are ＿＿ days in a week.
8 You haven't done very ＿＿ work.
9 There are not ＿＿ watches that keep perfect time.

Demonstrative and interrogative adjectives

There are also adjectives that 'point out' people, things, etc.

'I like *this* car.'   'I don't like *that* car.'

This and *these* are generally used for things that are near.
That and *those* are generally used for things that are further
away. *This* and *that* go with **singular** nouns. *These* and *those*
go with **plural** nouns.

   This car is old. (singular)

   That car is old. (singular)

   These cars are new. (plural)

   Those cars are new. (plural)

This, that, these, those are **demonstrative adjectives**.

There is one other kind of **adjective** that we must mention.

Interrogative adjectives are used with **nouns** to ask questions.

   What book are you reading now?

   What price are eggs today?

   Which boy can answer this question?

Which house do you live in?   *Whose* house is that?
                                 Whose cat is this?

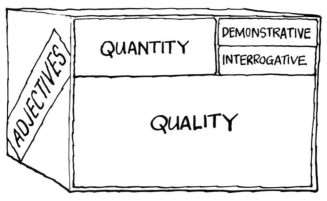

Exercises

A Complete the sentences with a **demonstrative adjective** in
each blank space.

Example: ＿＿ girl over there is beautiful.
Answer: That girl over there is beautiful.

1 I like ＿＿ flower.
2 I like ＿＿ flowers.
3 ＿＿ stars are in the east.
4 ＿＿ star is called the North Star.

5 Have you read ____ book I am reading?
6 Do you like ____ shoes I am wearing?
7 Will you give me ____ pen for ____ silver pencil?
8 ____ girls on the back seat are not working as hard as ____ girls on the front seat.
9 I bought ____ apples from ____ shop in the High Street.
10 ____ exercises we are doing on ____ page are more difficult than ____ exercises we did on page seven.

B Make the following phrases **plural.**

Example: that picture
Answer: those pictures

1 this door
2 that house
3 that big boy
4 this red apple
5 this new bicycle
6 that open window
7 that clever girl
8 that large fierce animal
9 this clean new book
10 that small yellow orange

C Make the following phrases **singular**.

1 those boys
2 these boys
3 those blue flowers
4 those black hens
5 these big dogs
6 these stupid boys
7 those large fierce animals
8 those dirty old books
9 these fine new bicycles
10 these bright red flowers

D Complete the sentences with an **interrogative adjective** in each blank space.

Example: ____ hand am I holding it in?
Answer: Which hand am I holding it in?

1 ____ bicycle is that?
2 ____ questions have you answered?
3 ____ time is it now?
4 ____ lesson do you like best?
5 ____ colour were the bottles on the wall?

E Pick out the **adjectives** in the following and say what kind of adjective each one is.

Example: Whose car is that red Peugeot?
Answer: Whose – interrogative adjective
          that – demonstrative adjective
          red – adjective of quality

1 There were four apples and two oranges on the plate.
2 This book is a good one.
3 A clever boy can soon do these exercises.
4 There are not many students in the class today.
5 I saw four birds in the tall tree.
6 We haven't much time to do this long exercise.
7 I wish my mother would buy me that big, new bicycle.
8 Which bicycle do you want?
9 What price is that bicycle?
10 Those four boys are brothers.
11 Nine green bottles were standing on this old wall.
12 When that song finished, there were no green bottles on the wall.
13 Whose pencil is on the desk?
14 What time are you going to the football match?
15 I think this new watch is a good one.

Lesson Nine

Verbs

Verbs are very important words.

We use verbs to say what people and things do. Verbs express an action.

The woodcutter *sat* on the bank. (What did he *do*?)
She *showed* him a gold axe. (What did she *do*?)
'That's mine,' *said* the woodcutter. (What did he *do*?)
The girls *go* to school every day. (What do they *do*?)
The man *opened* the box.
The bird *sings* at my window every morning.
The boys *ate* all the pudding.

Sometimes we use two words for a **verb**.

The poor woodcutter *was cutting* a piece of wood. (What *was* he *doing*?)

I *have lost* my axe. (What *has* he *done*?)

I *will give* you the gold axe and the silver axe. (What *will* she *do*?)

Some **verbs** don't express an action. They just say people or things *are* something. The chief of these is the verb *be* (*am, is, are, was, were*). These **verbs** often have an **adjective** after them.

The woodcutter *was* (verb) very *sad* (adjective).

The fairy asked the woodcutter why he *was* (verb) *unhappy* (adjective).

The fairy said, 'You *are* (verb) *honest* (adjective).'

Exercises

A Pick out the **verbs** expressing an action in the following sentences.

Example: The train stopped at a station.
Answer: stopped

1 The boy ran out of the house.
2 The girls danced.
3 The teacher gave us a lesson.
4 Birds sing.
5 The man smokes a pipe.
6 Fish swim in the sea.
7 The camel carries a load.
8 The train started again.
9 A car came to our door.
10 The sun shines.
11 I wrote a letter.

12 We learn grammar.
13 They speak English.
14 I received a letter this morning.
15 Wayne wrote the letter.
16 He put the letter in a letter-box.
17 Richard climbed a tree.
18 George shut the door.
19 I saw the teacher.
20 The pupils opened their books.

B Pick out the *two-word* **verbs** in these sentences.

Example: Is he writing a letter?
Answer: Is . . . writing

 1 The boy is writing.
 2 The girls are running.
 3 The teacher is giving us a lesson.
 4 The teacher will give us a lesson.
 5 The teacher has given us a lesson.
 6 The boy will run a race tomorrow.
 7 The camel is carrying a big load.
 8 The train has gone.
 9 The sun is shining.
10 I will write a letter.
11 I will write it in English.
12 I have written the letter.
13 They are speaking English.
14 They will speak English.
15 They have spoken English.
16 Richard is climbing a tree.
17 George has shut the door.
18 I have seen the teacher.
19 I will see the teacher.
20 The pupils have opened their books.
21 What is he doing?
22 What time will they arrive?

C Pick out the parts of the verb *be* in these sentences. Remember that this verb says what people or things are (or were).

Example: The man was very old.
Answer: was

1 Jeremy is tired.
2 Mary is very happy.
3 Those men are cold.
4 My cat is very pretty.
5 Those flowers are red.

6 I am tired.
7 Karen was unhappy.
8 The boys were hungry.
9 The teacher is kind.
10 The woodcutter was honest.

D Complete these sentences with parts of the verb *be*.

1 The woodcutter ____ very unhappy.
2 The fairy said, 'You ____ honest.'
3 I ____ glad that you are here.
4 My sister ____ very clever.
5 The flowers ____ pretty.

E Complete these sentences with verbs from the box. Use each verb once only.

| goes gave wrote jumps opened |
| painted bought cooks go washed |

1 The boy ____ the door.
2 The dog ____ over the gate every morning.
3 Tom ____ a good dinner every evening.
4 The woman ____ the dirty clothes.
5 The aeroplane ____ from Hong Kong to London.
6 I ____ these apples at the shop.
7 We ____ to school every day.
8 The chemist ____ the man a bottle of medicine.
9 The teacher ____ the words on the blackboard.
10 I ____ a picture on the paper.

F Make questions and give the answers for the pictures below. Underline all the **verbs** in your answers. We have done number 1 for you as an example.

Question: What is the boy doing?
Answer: He <u>is chopping</u> wood.

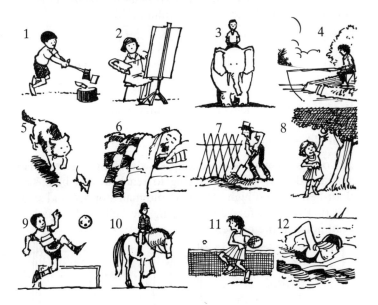

G Put a word from the box into the blank spaces to make two-word verbs.

was	am	are	has	were	have	is

1 The woodcutter _____ cutting a piece of wood.
2 I _____ doing my work.
3 The woodcutter _____ lost his axe.
4 The dog _____ jumped over the gate.
5 Tom's father _____ cooking a good dinner.
6 The woman _____ washed the dirty clothes.
7 I _____ done my work.

8 The fairy said, 'I ___ giving you the gold axe and the silver axe.'

9 We ___ drawing pictures on the paper.

10 The boys ___ playing in the playground.

H Pick out the **nouns**, the **adjectives** and the **verbs** in the following story. Write them in 3 columns like this:

Nouns	Adjectives	Verbs
gentleman street	old	was walking

We have filled in the words for the first sentence.

Poor old gentleman!

An old gentleman was walking slowly along a street. He saw a little boy who was trying to reach a door-bell. The door-bell was too high. The kind old man stopped and said, 'I'll ring the bell for you.' He rang the bell, and it made a loud noise in the house.

The little boy looked up at him and said, 'Now we'll run away. Come on!'

And the naughty boy ran round the corner. The old gentleman was still at the door when a big man came and opened it.

'Yes?' said the angry man. 'What do you want?'

Sentences and phrases

Sentences

When we want to express our thoughts we use a group of words. **A group of words that makes complete sense is a sentence**.

1 Tommy has a bicycle. (statement)

2 Where are you going? (question)

3 Open the door. (command)

The first sentence *tells* us something; it tells us that Tommy has a bicycle. It makes a **statement**.

The second sentence doesn't tell us anything; it *asks* something; it asks where someone is going. It is a **question**. The answer to this question will be a statement.

The third sentence is neither a statement nor a question. It doesn't give us some information (like a statement), and it doesn't ask for information (like a question). It orders someone to do something. It is a **command**.

So, you see, a sentence can do one of three things.
1 Make a statement to tell us something.
2 Ask a question.
3 Give a command.

Some **statements** can be turned into **questions** and some **questions** can be turned into **statements**, by changing the order of the words. Here are some examples:

Statement	*Question*
That is Mary's bicycle.	Is that Mary's bicycle?
John can speak French.	Can John speak French?
You have had your lesson.	Have you had your lesson?
The boy will do the work.	Will the boy do the work?

And here are some examples of **commands**:
Look at this sentence.
Be quiet!
Please come here.
Come here, please.
Jane, answer the question.
Answer the question, Jane.

Phrases

You may have a group of words that makes sense but not *complete* sense, for example: *into the house*; *at nine o'clock*; *for eighty pence*.

Groups of words like these are **phrases**. A sentence has a **verb** in it; a phrase hasn't. You can turn a **phrase** into a **sentence** by adding other words to it, but one of the words that you add must be a **verb**. Let us make the **phrases** in our example into **sentences** by adding something (including a verb) to them.

John *went* into the house.

I *left* home at nine o'clock.

George *bought* the book for eighty pence.

Exercises

A Make two columns with the headings **sentences** and **phrases**. Then put each group of words below under the right heading. For a **sentence** you need a capital letter and a full stop (or '?' or '!'). We have done the first two for you.

Sentences	Phrases
1 We saw the boy.	2 at the chemist's

1 we saw the boy	10 come here
2 at the chemist's	11 from my father
3 in the garden	12 sit down
4 open the door	13 through the window
5 across the garden	14 where are my books
6 at our school	15 did you see Margaret
7 an honest man	16 on Tuesday morning
8 near the school	17 please don't say that
9 on my desk	

B Add words to turn these phrases into sentences.

Example: beside the river
Answer: Let's walk beside the river. (Or any other addition that contains a **verb**)

1 a few years ago	4 after six o'clock
2 every summer	5 on page sixteen
3 in the garden	6 by Friday night

51

7 with a hammer
8 into the sea
9 near the railway station
10 through the window
11 in his pocket

12 along the High Street
13 with you and me
14 with Jeremy and Richard
15 on the blackboard

C Here is a little story. Copy the sentences that have brackets [ ] after them, and in the brackets write S (for **statement**) or Q (for **question**) or C (for **command**). We have filled in the first pair of brackets for you.

The duke and the farmer

The Duke of Wellington was very rich. [S] He had a lot of land in a beautiful part of England. [   ] Next to the Duke's land there was a farm. [   ] The Duke wanted to buy the farm and add its fields to his land. [   ]

'Go and see Farmer Jackson,' [   ] he said to his agent. 'Try to buy his farm for me.' [   ]

After a few weeks, the agent came to the Duke. [   ]
'I've bought the farm for you,' [   ] he said.
'How much did you pay for it?' [   ] the Duke asked.
'I got it for £30,000,' [   ] the agent said. 'The real value
of Farmer Jackson's land is £40,000. [   ] Wasn't it a bargain?' [   ]
'Is the land really worth £40,000? [   ] Then tell me this.
[   ] How did you get it for £30,000?' [   ]
'Farmer Jackson is in trouble,' [   ] the agent answered.
'He needs the money at once. [   ] He had to sell his farm
cheaply.'[   ]
'Go back to Farmer Jackson at once,' [   ] said the Duke.
'Give him the £10,000. [   ] If he needs the money, we must
give him the real value of his land. [   ] I don't want a
bargain that comes from another man's trouble.' [   ]

D Turn these **questions** into **statements**.

Example: Was Jackson the owner of the farm?
Answer: Jackson was the owner of the farm.

1 Was Jackson's farm next to the Duke's land?
2 Were there fields on Farmer Jackson's land?
3 Was the price of the farm £30,000?
4 Was the real value of the farm £40,000?
5 Was £30,000 a bargain?
6 Was Farmer Jackson in trouble?
7 Was the Duke sorry for Farmer Jackson?

E Turn the following **statements** into **questions**.

Example: The farm is worth £40,000.
Answer: Is the farm worth £40,000?

1 The real value of the farm was £40,000.
2 Farmer Jackson was in trouble.
3 The fields were round the farm.

4 The farm was next to the Duke's land.
5 The Duke will give the farmer £40,000.
6 That was a fair price for the farm.
7 Farmer Jackson was very glad.

F Make **commands** using these words. Use them in any order, and add more words if you need them.

Example: Farm, for me, buy.
Answer: Buy the farm for me.

1 Door, John, open.
2 Mary, book, to me, quickly, bring.
3 At home, exercise, do, carefully.
4 Tomorrow, homework, here, bring.
5 Talking, stop, now, and, work, begin.
6 On page 25, all the questions, do.
7 Your name, top of paper, write.
8 For me, at post office, post, letters.
9 Your exercise book, to school, bring, tomorrow.
10 Richard, ball, kick, into the goal.

G Write out 3 **statements**, 3 **questions** and 3 **commands** of your own. Don't copy them from this lesson.

The subject of a sentence

Here are seven sentences:

A	B
The Duke of Wellington	wanted to buy the farm.
I	can do these exercises.
The poor woodcutter	lost his axe.
This book	belongs to me.
The boy	laughed.
A little boy in a blue shirt and shorts	ran down the street.
The workman	is unhappy.

You will notice that each sentence is divided into two parts by a line and the parts are marked A and B.

The subject

Part A (*The Duke of Wellington, I, The poor woodcutter, This book, The boy, A little boy in a blue shirt and shorts, The workman*) contains the person or thing we are talking about in the sentence. We call this the **subject** of the sentence.

The word or group of words that we speak about in a sentence is called the subject. The subject is the 'doer' of the action.

You want to practise finding the **subject** of the sentence. Why? Because the **subject** is the word or group of words that:

1 changes place when we make a question:
   The girl is clever.   Is *the girl* clever?
   subject   **subject**

2 decides the form of the **verb** in some cases:
   Is the girl clever?   *Are the girls* clever?
    subject   **subject**

The predicate

Part B (*wanted to buy the farm, can do these exercises, lost his axe, belongs to me, laughed, ran down the street, is unhappy*) is what we say about the subject. We call that part of the sentence the **predicate**. The predicate can be one word, or it can be several words.

The predicate of a sentence is the word or group of words that tells us something about the subject.

There is generally a **noun** or a **pronoun** (Lesson 13) in the **subject** (*Duke of Wellington, I, woodcutter, book, boy, workman*).

There is always a **verb** in the **predicate** (*wanted, can do, lost, belongs, laughed, ran, is*).

There is an easy way to find out the **subject** of a sentence.
First pick out the **verb** and ask, 'Who?' or 'What?'

Who?/What? → **verb** = **subject**

Look at these examples:
This book belongs to me.
What → belongs? = This book (**subject**)
A little boy ran down the street.
Who → ran? = A little boy (**subject**)

Exercises

A Pick out the **subject** of each of the following sentences:

1 Birds fly. (Ask: What?)
2 Fish swim. (Ask: What?)
3 The pupil reads a book. (Ask: Who?)
4 The cat caught a mouse. (Ask: What?)
5 Henry opened the door. (Ask: Who?)
6 Margaret Lee goes to school.
7 A man went into the chemist's shop.
8 The chemist opened the bottle.
9 The medicine has cured your headache.
10 A poor woodcutter was cutting wood.
11 His axe fell into the water.
12 The fairy showed him a silver axe.
13 I can give you the gold axe and the silver axe.
14 An old gentleman was walking along the street.
15 The naughty boy ran round the corner.
16 The man was very angry.
17 The real value of Farmer Jackson's land is £40,000.
18 The girl is going to the shops.
19 The moon gives less light than the sun.
20 The Duke's agent took £10,000 and gave it to Farmer
Jackson.

B Add **predicates** to these **subjects**.

1 The fairy . . . .
2 The woodcutter . . . .
3 He . . . .
4 My friend in London . . . .
5 The horses . . . .
6 The driver of the train . . . .
7 The chemist . . . .
8 Flowers . . . .
9 A big red-faced man . . . .
10 The blackboard . . . .

C Give **subjects** to these **predicates**.

1 . . . . is in the garden.
2 . . . . has lost his knife.
3 . . . . sing.
4 . . . . opened the door.
5 . . . . wanted to buy a farm.
6 . . . . went into the shop.
7 . . . . sat at the back of the class.
8 . . . . is making the flowers grow.
9 . . . . will feed the hens.
10 . . . . went slowly out of the station.
11 . . . . answered all the questions.
12 . . . . sells butter, sugar and tea.
13 . . . . visits Trinidad three times a year.
14 . . . . laid an egg
15 . . . . have lost all their leaves.

Lesson Twelve

The object of a verb

If I said to you,
  'The dog killed.
  He killed yesterday,' or 'This shopkeeper sells',

you would be puzzled. You would say, 'Go on. Finish the sentence. Tell us what the shopkeeper sells. Tell us what the dog killed. Those verbs *sell* and *kill* don't make sense by themselves. You must put something after them to make sense.'

So I say,
  'This shopkeeper   'The dog killed a rat.
  sells bicycles.'   He killed it yesterday.'

'Oh yes,' you say at once, 'that makes sense.'

The word *bicycles* is the **object** of the verb *sell*.
The words *a rat* and *it* are the **objects** of the verb *kill*.

The object of a verb is a noun or pronoun which tells us the person or thing that the action of the verb happened to. The object is the 'receiver' of the action.

We found the **subject** of the sentence by saying the question word *who*? (or *what*?) *before* the verb (Lesson 11). We can find the **object** by saying the question word *what*? (or *who(m)*?) *after* the verb.

Who?/What? → **verb**	= **subject**
verb → what?	= **object**

To find the subject and object of this sentence:

The shopkeeper sells bicycles.

Who	→ sells?	= The shopkeeper (**subject**)
	sells → what?	= bicycles (**object**)

Here are some more examples:

The rat bit the dog.

What	→ bit?	= The rat (**subject**)
	bit → what?	= the dog (**object**)

The dog killed the rat.

What	→ killed?	= The dog (**subject**)
	killed → what?	= the rat (**object**)

Transitive Verbs

Verbs that have an **object** (some verbs don't) are **transitive verbs**. 'Transitive' comes from a Latin word that means 'going over'. The action of *killing* 'goes over' from the dog to the rat. The action of *selling* 'goes over' from the shopkeeper to the bicycles.

In the sentence *The rat bit the dog*, the action of *biting* goes from the rat to the dog. The rat is the 'doer' of the action; the dog is the 'receiver' of the action. In the sentence *The dog killed the rat*, the action of *killing* goes from the dog to the rat. The dog is the 'doer' of the action; the rat is the 'receiver' of the action. Both sentences have **objects**: the verbs *bite* and *kill* are **transitive verbs**.

Verbs that take objects are called transitive verbs.

Intransitive Verbs

But there are some verbs that don't have objects, because sometimes the action doesn't 'go over' from one person or thing to another person or thing. Consider these sentences for example:

The dog growled.

The rat died.

The action of *growling* starts and ends with the dog. It doesn't 'go over' to anything else. The action of *dying* begins and ends with the rat.

If you say, *growled what?*, *died what?*, you can't get a sensible answer. These verbs don't have an object. They are **intransitive verbs**.

Verbs that don't take objects are called intransitive verbs.

Exercises

A Pick out the **objects** in these sentences.

1 Cows eat grass.
2 Richard cut his finger.
3 The teacher taught his class.
4 John read a book.
5 Margaret sang a song.
6 The pupils read their books.
7 The policeman caught the thief.
8 Mr Brown bought a car.
9 The train left the station.
10 A supermarket sells tea.
11 We play football.
12 George ate an apple.
13 My mother cooked the dinner.
14 My sister opened the door.
15 The men have finished their work.
16 Eric Lee has scored a goal.
17 Henry is writing a letter.
18 Who rang the bell?
19 Have you seen my new bicycle? (The verb is *have seen*.)
20 Can you open this box?

B Pick out the **subjects** and the **objects** of the verbs in the following sentences. Remember the plan:

Who?/What? → verb   = **subject**
verb → what? = **object**

Draw three columns and write the **subject**, **verb** and **object** of each sentence in the correct column. We have filled in the first sentence for you.

Subject	Verb	Object
The medicine	cured	my headache

1 The medicine cured my headache.
2 The woodcutter lost his old axe.
3 The old gentleman saw a little boy.
4 The boy couldn't read his book.
5 Henry wrote a letter.
6 That man has written a book.
7 The girls sang songs.
8 Henry has bought a football.
9 The woodcutter was cutting a piece of wood.
10 The Duke of Wellington wanted a farm.
11 The agent paid £30,000.
12 The Duke sent £10,000.
13 The farmer didn't have money.
14 The farmer grows potatoes and corn.
15 Henry ate an apple and an orange.
16 The teacher marked all our exercises.
17 At the farm I saw some cows, sheep and horses.
18 The cows, sheep and horses ate a lot of grass.
19 The poor woodcutter saw a beautiful fairy.
20 In her hand she held a gold axe.

C Pick out the **verbs** in the following sentences. Put the **transitive verbs** in one column and the **intransitive verbs** in another column. We have done the first two verbs for you.

Transitive	Intransitive
hurt	cried

1 The little boy hurt his foot.
2 He cried bitterly.
3 The sun is shining.
4 The boys saw the football match.
5 Richard slept until nine o'clock.
6 Cotton grows in Egypt.
7 The children fed the animals.

8 The train started.
9 Birds fly.
10 George is working hard.
11 We live in Bridgetown.
12 The water is boiling.
13 Clouds are passing across the sky.
14 The boys like their lessons.
15 The butcher sells meat.
16 The farmer's wife went to the dairy.
17 Wood burns easily.
18 The children are sitting still at their desks.
19 Please give me those flowers.
20 I will go to Hong Kong next week.

D Read this short story.

The joke

Sir William Thompson was very deaf, but he always pretended that he could hear everything. One evening he *invited* several friends to dinner. While they *were sitting* at the table, one of the friends *told* a funny story. Everyone *laughed*. William laughed very loudly too. Then he said, 'That was a very funny joke, but I *know* a funnier one. Would you like to hear it?' They all said they would, so William *began* his story. When it *ended*, everyone laughed louder than before. William *smiled* happily. But he *didn't know* the reason for their laughter. He *had told* the same story.

Ten of the verbs in that story are printed in italics. Draw four columns like this in your exercise book.

1. Subject	2. Verb	3. Object	4. Kind of Verb
he	invited	several friends	T

Write in column 2 each of the **verbs** in italics. Write the

subject of each verb in column 1. Write the **object** (if there is one) in column 3. And in column 4 put T if the verb is **transitive**, or I if it is **intransitive**. We have filled in the columns for the first verb for you.

The complement

'That man is' isn't a complete sentence. It needs something to make it complete. Perhaps: 'That man is a detective.' We say that *detective* is not an object of *is*. The man doesn't do anything to the detective. He *is* the detective: *man = detective*. We give a special name to words or phrases which complete a sentence after **verbs** like *be, seem, become*. They are **complements**.

E Complete these sentences by adding a **complement.**

Example: The teacher's mother seems ____.
Answer: The teacher's mother seems old.

1 Anne Carter is ____.
2 She was ____, but now she is ____.
3 Today is ____, and tomorrow will be ____.
4 That old lady feeds the birds. She seems ____.
5 Mary was ____, but she has become ____.
6 Is your brother ____, or is he ____?

Pronouns

Look at this story:

John Brown said that *John Brown* was hungry. Mary Brown said that *Mary Brown* was hungry, too. When their mother heard that *John and Mary* were hungry, *their mother* gave *John and Mary* a piece of cake each. *John and Mary* thanked *their mother* for *the piece of cake* and *John and Mary* ate *the piece of cake*. Then John said, '*John* thanks *his mother. John* isn't hungry now,' and Mary said, '*Mary* thanks *her mother. Mary* isn't hungry now.' Their mother said, 'Did *John and Mary* enjoy *the cake*?' and *John and Mary* said together, '*John and Mary* enjoyed *the cake* very much.'

It sounds funny, doesn't it? I'm sure you can see why. It's because we keep repeating the nouns *John* and *Mary* and *mother* and *piece of cake*. Now let's try again, and this time, instead of always using these nouns, we will use other words that stand for them. We'll mark all the words that we use instead of the nouns.

John Brown said that *he* was hungry. Mary Brown said that *she* was hungry, too. When their mother heard that *they* were hungry, *she* gave *them* a piece of cake each. *They* thanked *her* for *it* and *they* ate *it*. Then John said, '(*I*) Thank *you*. *I*'m not hungry now,' and Mary said, '(*I*) Thank *you*. *I*'m not hungry now.' Their mother said, 'Did *you* enjoy *it*?' And *they* said together, '*We* enjoyed *it* very much.'

That sounds better, doesn't it? We have used **pronouns,** words that we use instead of the nouns. The pronouns in that story are the words *I, you, he, she, we, they, them, her, him, it*.

Words that stand instead of nouns are called pronouns.

Exercise

Pick out the **pronouns** in the following.

 1 John is a boy. He is at home.
 2 Mary is a girl. She is in the class.
 3 They are brother and sister.
 4 We know them very well.
 5 They stayed with us last year.
 6 John is a clever boy. I like him.
 7 Mary is our friend. She is twelve years old. We like her.
 8 They have a bicycle. It is yellow.
 9 They have asked me to visit them next year.
10 They live in Kingston. It is a big city.
11 Do you like these flowers? They are out of the garden.
12 I read that book. It is very interesting.
13 Show me how to do this exercise.
14 Don't you know how to do it?
15 I don't understand how to do it.

Gender of nouns and pronouns

In the story about John and Mary, when we used **pronouns** instead of **nouns**, we sometimes used *he, him* and at other times *she, her*. Of course you know when to use *he, him* and when to use *she, her*. The pronouns *he* and *him* are used when they stand for nouns like *man* or *boy*; that is, for males. The pronouns *she, her* are used when they stand for nouns like *woman* or *girl*; that is, for females.

In grammar we say that the forms *he* and *she* (or *him* and *her*) show a difference of **gender**.

Words that stand for males are masculine gender. So the nouns *man, boy, son, king, prince*, etc., and the pronouns *he* and *him* are **masculine** gender.

Words that stand for females are feminine gender. The nouns *woman, girl, daughter, queen, princess*, etc., and the pronouns *she* and *her* are **feminine** gender.

Words that stand for things are neutral gender. (Neutral means neither masculine nor feminine.) So the nouns *book, house, river, tree, city*, etc., and the pronoun *it* are **neutral** gender.

Sometimes the **pronouns** used for animals are **neutral** gender.

Where is the cat? *It* is on the mat.
Where is the dog? *It* is in the garden.

The pronouns *I, me, you, we, us* can be either **masculine** or **feminine**. The pronouns *they* and *them* may be **masculine** or **feminine** or **neutral**.

The boys have just come home. Ask *them* if *they* want their dinner. (**masculine**)
The girls have been to the cinema. Ask *them* if *they* enjoyed the picture. (**feminine**)
The apple-trees are covered with blossom. *They* will have plenty of apples on *them* in the autumn. (**neutral**)

Exercises

A Answer these questions.

1 What is the gender of **nouns** or **pronouns** that stand for male persons?
2 What is the gender of **nouns** or **pronouns** that stand for female persons?
3 What is the gender of **nouns** or **pronouns** that stand for things or animals?

B

1 Write down four **nouns** in the **masculine** gender and four in the **feminine** gender.
2 Write down two **pronouns** in the **feminine** gender and two in the **masculine** gender.
3 Write down ten **nouns** or **pronouns** in the **neutral** gender.
4 Which two **pronouns** can be **masculine**, **feminine** and **neutral**?
5 Which **pronoun** is only **neutral** gender?

C Give the **feminine** of the following **nouns** and **pronouns**.

Example: grandfather (masculine)
Answer: grandmother (feminine)

1 he	6 husband	11 policeman	16 nephew
2 him	7 father	12 actor	17 uncle
3 boy	8 son	13 lion	18 duke
4 king	9 brother	14 gentleman	19 hero
5 prince	10 man	15 Mr	20 tiger

D Give the **masculine** of the following **nouns** and **pronouns**.

1 her	6 woman	11 actress	16 lioness
2 she	7 girl	12 lady	17 princess
3 queen	8 sister	13 niece	18 mother
4 wife	9 heroine	14 duchess	19 tigress
5 daughter	10 policewoman	15 aunt	20 Mrs

Lesson Fifteen

Pronouns:
singular and plural, persons

You have just seen how useful the **pronouns** are. The pronouns you have looked at in Lessons 13 and 14 are used instead of **nouns** that mean persons or animals or things. We call them **personal pronouns**.

Singular and plural

The pronouns *I, me, he, she , him, her* are used for only one person. So they are **singular**.

The pronouns *we, us, they, them* are used for more than one person. They are **plural**.

You is both singular and plural.
    You are a good boy (one boy, **singular**).
    You are good boys (more than one boy, **plural**).

We call *it* a **personal pronoun** too, but we use it to mean an animal or a thing. The **plural** of *it* is *they* or *them*.

Persons

You have met the word *persons*, of course, meaning *people*.
But in grammar, person (**first person**, **second person**, **third person**) has another meaning.

The 1st person is the person speaking.

The 2nd person is the person spoken to.

The 3rd person is the person spoken about.

Richard is looking through the window. The teacher is pointing at *him*. *They* are pupils; *she* teaches *them*. Richard's mother thinks *he* is in the classroom – but *she* is wrong.

Impersonal subject

There is also another use for *it*, as the **impersonal subject** in such sentences as,

   It is raining.

It was a fine day yesterday.
It's a long way from here to London.

Exercises

A Pick out the **pronouns** in these sentences. Write **singular** or **plural** after each of them.

Example: They are big horses.
Answer: They – plural.

1 He is playing football.
2 She is watching him.
3 They don't see the teacher.
4 He sees them.
5 You are all working hard.
6 You are the boy I saw playing football. ·
7 We have a lesson every day.
8 Tell us what you told her.
9 It is hot today.
10 If you don't understand this lesson, ask me about it.

B What do we mean by (a) the **1st person**, (b) the **2nd person**, (c) the **3rd person**?

C Pick out the **pronouns** in these sentences. Say what **person** each one is.

Example: I love her.
Answer: I – 1st person; her – 3rd person.

1 You must do the work.
2 He is not working very hard.
3 We come to the class every day, and the teacher teaches us.
4 They can do it, if they try.

5 I asked him to come and see me.
6 She asked me to bring the book to her.
7 You can sit next to them.
8 She doesn't like me and I don't like her.
9 We don't like them and they don't like us.
10 You don't like him and he doesn't like you.

Lesson Sixteen

Pronouns: subject and object

In Lessons 11 and 12 we talked about **subjects** and **objects**:

Subject	Verb	Object
The boy	kicked	the football
The cat	caught	a mouse

In English (but not in all languages), **nouns** always have the same form whether they are the subject or the object.

Subject	Verb	Object
The boy	hit	the dog
The dog	bit	the boy

As you see, the nouns *boy* and *dog* can be **subjective** or **objective** without any change of form. As **subject** or as **object** they are b–o–y and d–o–g. But **pronouns** are different. With most of them there is one form for the **subject** and another form for the **object**. *I* is subjective; *me* is objective. *He* is subjective; *him* is objective, and so on. For example:

Subject	Verb	Object
I	know	the boy
The boy	knows	*me*
He	knows	the teacher
The teacher	knows	*him*
She	knows	the teacher
The teacher	knows	*her*
We	know	the teacher
The teacher	knows	*us*
They	know	the teacher
The teacher	knows	*them*

You and *it* are the same whether they are the **subject** or the **object**.

Subject	Verb	Object
You	hit	it
It	bit	you

This table will help you to remember what you have learned about pronouns.

			Personal Pronouns	
			Subjective	Objective
1st Person	Singular		I	me
	Plural		we	us
2nd Person	Singular		you	
	Plural			
3rd person	Singular	Masculine	he	him
		Feminine	she	her
		Neutral	it	
	Plural		they	them

Exercises

A Pick out the **pronouns** in these sentences. Write **subject** or **object** after each.

Example: They took us in their car.
Answer: They – subject; us – object

1 I taught him at school.
2 He helped us with this exercise.
3 She will see them tomorrow.
4 You broke that window; I saw you.
5 It will cost a lot of money to mend it.
6 I asked her to come and see me.
7 We couldn't do the exercise until the teacher told us how to do it.
8 They played us at football, and we beat them.
9 He scored a goal, and we all cheered him.
10 She did the exercise well. When I had marked it, I praised her.

B Divide these sentences into **subject**, **verb**, **object** like this:

Subject	Verb	Object
I	taught	you

and then underline each **pronoun** on your paper. We have answered the first one in the example.

1 I taught you.
2 He saw me.
3 She knows us.
4 We know her.
5 They praised him.
6 He thanked them.
7 She hit the ball.
8 He threw it.
9 It broke a window.
10 They blamed him.

C Change the **pronouns** in these sentences from **singular** to **plural**. In some cases you will have to change the **verb** too.

Example: He likes me.
Answer: They like us.

1 I come to school every day.
2 He is hungry.
3 She can sing very well.
4 The teacher gives me an English lesson.
5 The teacher asked him a question.
6 I asked her to sing 'Ten Green Bottles'.
7 He told me a story.
8 You are working hard.
9 I am English; what is he?
10 He doesn't see me.

D Write out these sentences, but with **pronouns** instead of the words printed in *italics*. You will need to change the **verb** too in 17, 18, 19 and 20

1 *John* is a boy.
2 *Margaret* is a girl.
3 *John and Margaret* met the teacher.
4 *Mrs Smith, the teacher*, gave *John* a lesson.
5 Margaret is a nice girl. *My wife and I* like *Margaret*.
6 Here is my bicycle. *My bicycle* is black.
7 *Mr Jones, the teacher*, said, 'Give *the teacher* your book.'
8 The teacher said to John and Margaret, 'Have *John and Margaret* done this exercise?'
9 The lesson is easy. *Mrs Smith, the teacher*, explained *the lesson*.
10 Mr Jones, the teacher, spoke to John and Margaret. *The teacher* asked *John and Margaret* to come and see *the teacher*.
11 Tom saw Mary. *Tom* spoke to *Mary*.
12 Mary saw Tom. *Mary* spoke to *Tom*.

13 Tom and Mary saw Mrs Robinson. *Tom and Mary* spoke to *Mrs Robinson*.

14 Mrs Robinson saw Tom and Mary. *Mrs Robinson* spoke to *Tom and Mary*.

15 Mr Sangster met Carl and Linda. *Mr Sangster* shook hands with *Carl and Linda*.

16 Linda and Carl met Mr Sangster. *Linda and Carl* shook hands with *Mr Sangster*.

17 Linda and Carl said to Mr Sangster, 'Is *Mr Sangster* pleased to see *Linda and Carl*?'

18 'My name is Henry. What is your name?'
'My name is George, and *George* is very pleased to meet *Henry*.'

19 My name is Grace. What is your name?'
'My name is Margaret, and *Margaret* is very pleased to meet *Grace*.'

20 'My name is Linda. What are your names?' 'Our names are Jane and Elizabeth, and *Jane and Elizabeth* are very pleased to meet *Linda*. Is *Linda* pleased to meet *Jane and Elizabeth*?'

E Here is another story. Write it out again, but use **pronouns** instead of **nouns** where **pronouns** are better.

Isaac Newton's egg

Three hundred years ago, Isaac Newton was a great man of science. No man was a greater thinker, but Newton was very absent-minded about small matters when Newton was thinking about a problem. One morning Newton got up very early because Newton was working on a very difficult problem. Newton was thinking about the problem so deeply that Newton would not leave the problem to go to break-fast. But Mary, his housekeeper, thought Newton needed food, so the housekeeper took a pan of water and an egg to his study. The housekeeper wanted to boil the egg and stay with Newton until Newton ate the egg.

But Newton wanted to be alone, and Newton said, 'Mary can leave the egg with Newton, and Newton will boil the egg.' The housekeeper put the egg on the table beside Newton's watch, and the housekeeper said, 'Isaac must boil the egg for four minutes and then the egg will be ready.'

Then the housekeeper left the room. But the house-keeper was afraid that Newton might forget to boil the egg. So the housekeeper returned about an hour later. The housekeeper found Newton standing by the fireplace. Newton had put the watch in the saucepan, and Newton was boiling the watch. Newton was holding the egg in his hand. But Newton was still thinking about his problem.

Adverbs

We saw in Lesson 6 that **adjectives** are used with **nouns.**
Other words go with **verbs. The words that we use with verbs
are called adverbs**.

Some **adverbs** tell how an action is done. For example:
   The old gentleman *walked* (verb) *slowly* (adverb) along
   the street.
   The little boy *ran* (verb) *quickly* (adverb).
   The woodcutter *sat* (verb) *sadly* (adverb) by the side of the
   river.
These adverbs are called **adverbs of manner**.

Adverbs are often formed by adding *-ly* to an **adjective**.
   The boy is a *quick* (adjective) runner.
   The boy runs *quickly* (adverb).
   The old gentleman was a *slow* (adjective) walker.
   The old gentleman walked *slowly* (adverb).
   The little boy's behaviour was *bad* (adjective).
   The little boy behaved *badly* (adverb).

Note that when the adjective ends in *-y*, the adverb changes the *-y* to *-i*
> The bird sang a *merry* (adjective) song.
> The bird sang *merrily* (adverb).

But there are some adverbs that are not formed like this. Here are some examples:
> John is a *hard* (adjective) worker.
> John works *hard* (adverb).
> This is a *fast* (adjective) train.
> It goes very *fast* (adverb).
> The little girl's behaviour was *good* (adjective).
> The little girl behaved *well* (adverb).

Adverbs usually follow the **verb** they go with; **adjectives** usually come before the **noun** they go with.

A few **adverbs** tell us *when* (not how) an action was done.
> The woodcutter lost his axe *yesterday*. (When did he lose it?)
> We must come to school *tomorrow*. (When must we come to school?)

These adverbs are called **adverbs of time**.

A few **adverbs** tell us *where* an action happened.
> I sat down *there*. (Where did I sit down?)

These adverbs are called **adverbs of place**.

We use an **adverb** with a **verb** to tell how, when or where an action happens. We say the **adverb** *modifies* the **verb**.

Exercises

A Find the **adverbs** in these sentences.

Example: You'll do this exercise carefully, won't you?
Answer: carefully

 1 The birds sang sweetly.
 2 The man spoke slowly.
 3 The children played happily.
 4 The boy wrote his exercise badly.
 5 The woodcutter looked sadly at the river.
 6 When he saw his axe, he smiled happily.
 7 Every soldier fought bravely.
 8 You must work hard if you want to do this exercise correctly. (2 adverbs)
 9 Richard ate his breakfast fast and then ran quickly to school. (2 adverbs)
10 The school team played well and won their game easily. (2 adverbs)
11 Come here.
12 Why did you go there?
13 I did the work yesterday.
14 You didn't do it well; you must do it carefully now. (3 adverbs)
15 The girl shouted suddenly, 'The car is here!' (2 adverbs)
16 The teacher spoke clearly, and we understood her easily. (2 adverbs)
17 George worked hard and did the exercise well today. (3 adverbs)
18 The child opened the door of the cage and the bird flew out.
19 He didn't know the bird would fly away.
20 You came here late today; you must come early tomorrow. (5 adverbs)

B Use **adverbs** from the list in the box to fill the blank spaces. Say whether your adverb shows the **manner**, or **time**, or **place** of the action. We have completed number 1 for you.

well	quickly	carefully	brightly	tomorrow	tonight	
hard	loudly	here	fast	today	slowly	carelessly

1 The boy wrote *quickly (manner)*.
2 You are working too ____.
3 I will do the work ____.
4 Open the door ____.
5 Come ____. I want to speak to you.
6 I saw Jane ____ and I shall see her again ____.
7 Carmen drove the car ____ along the wide road but ____ in the crowded streets.
8 It was a beautiful day, the sun was shining ____, the birds were singing ____ and the children were playing in the field.
9 Mary is a good singer; I didn't know she sang so ____.
10 Learning English is hard work, but I want to learn it and so I will work ____.

C Read this story.

Fire! fire!

Mr King was writing busily in his big room. His son Ian rushed excitedly into the room and shouted loudly, 'Fire, fire! The kitchen is on fire!'

Mr King got up quickly, and he and Ian ran as fast as they could to the kitchen.

'Look there,' shouted Ian, and he pointed to the flames. He had carelessly left a towel near the stove and it was burning fiercely.

Mr King saw a big pan of boiling water on the top of the stove. 'You silly boy,' he said. 'Why didn't you throw that on the burning towel? That would have put it out quickly.'

'Oh no,' said the boy, slowly. 'That water would be useless; it's hot water.'

Draw four columns like this:

1 Nouns	2 Verbs	3 Adjectives	4 Adverbs
Mr King room	was writing	big (his)	busily (M)

Into the first column put all the **nouns** in the story. Put all the **verbs** into the second column. Into the third one put all the **adjectives**. And put all the **adverbs** into the fourth one. If the **adverb** tells *how* the action was done, put 'M' (for **manner**) after it. If it tells *when*, put 'T' (for **time**). If it tells *where*, put 'P' (for **place**). We have done the first sentence for you.

Prepositions. Adverb phrases. Adjective phrases

Let's open the next box and see what comes out. Here they come: *to, with, on, in*. They include some of the shortest words in the language, but sometimes they are the most difficult to use.

You will generally hear or see them used with a **noun** or **pronoun** to make a phrase (a group of words without a verb). For example: *at* my house; *in* your school; *with* you. Here are some more examples:

Preposition		Noun or pronoun
in	your	pocket
over	the	wall
through	the	window
to		him
round	the	house
into	the	garden
towards	the	door

These phrases often do the work of an **adverb**: they tell how, when or where an action was done. We call them **adverb phrases**.

The soldiers fought *bravely* (adverb of manner).
The soldiers fought *with great bravery* (adverb phrase).
He came *yesterday* (adverb of time).
He came *at four o'clock* (adverb phrase).
She sat *there* (adverb of place).
She sat *in the corner* (adverb phrase).

At other times they do the work of an **adjective**: they limit the meaning of a **noun**. These phrases are called **adjective phrases**. Here are some examples:

A *dirty* (adjective) boy opened the door.
A boy *with a dirty face* (adjective phrase) opened the door.
I like a *corner* (adjective) seat in the train.
I like a seat *in the corner* (adjective phrase).

Here are some more examples of **adjective phrases**:

The children *of the village* go to this school.
The picture *on the wall* shows Westminster Abbey.
The view *through the open window* is very pretty.
The boy *with me* is Richard.

Sometimes the same group of words may be an **adverb phrase** or an **adjective phrase**. It all depends on the work it is doing. Look at these phrases:

The view *through the open window* is very pretty.
This is an **adjective phrase** because it qualifies, or limits the meaning of, the noun *view*.

The bird flew *through the open window*.
An **adverb phrase** because it modifies, or limits the meaning of, the verb *flew*. It tells where it flew.

The class *in this room* is learning English.
An **adjective phrase**. It qualifies the noun *class*.

We learn English *in this room*.
An **adverb phrase**. It modifies the verb *learn*.

The bell *at eleven o'clock* tells us that the lesson is finished.
Adjective phrase. It qualifies the noun *bell*.

They ring the bell *at eleven o'clock* to tell us that the lesson is finished.
Adverb phrase. It modifies the verb *ring*.

There is just one more thing to notice. **After a preposition, the pronoun in the phrase is always the object pronoun**.

He came with *them*.
He will sit between you and *me*.
This letter was written by *him*.
He bought the house from *us*.

We say that the **preposition** *governs* the **noun** or **pronoun** it goes with.

Exercises

A Here is another short story. The **prepositions** in it are
printed in *italics*. Say which **noun** or **pronoun** each governs.
We have done the first sentence of the story as an example.

Preposition	*Noun or pronoun*
in	London
in	poverty

A life for a life

Richard Savage was once living *in* London *in* great poverty.
To earn a little money he had written the story *of* his life,
but not many copies *of* the book had been sold *in* the shops.
Savage was still very poor. Because he couldn't buy enough
food, he became very ill. But *after* a time, *owing to* the skill
of the doctor, he got well again. *After* a week or two the
doctor sent a bill *to* Savage *for* his visits, but poor Savage
hadn't any money and couldn't pay it. The doctor waited
for another month and sent the bill again. But still no
money came. *After* several weeks he sent it *to* him again,
asking *for* his money. *In* the end he came *to* Savage's house
and asked him *for* payment. He said to Savage, 'You know
you owe your life *to* me and I expected some gratitude *from*
you.'

'I agree,' said Savage, 'that I owe my life *to* you. To
prove *to* you that I am not ungrateful *for* your work I will
give my life *to* you.' *With* these words he handed *to* him two
volumes *with* the words 'The Life of Richard Savage' *on* the
cover.

B Put **prepositions** in the blank spaces.

1 Savage lived ＿＿ London ＿＿ great poverty.
2 He wrote the story ＿＿ his life.

3 He was still ___ need ___ money, and he couldn't pay ___ enough food.

4 ___ a time, as a result ___ his lack ___ food, he became ill.

5 He got better, thanks ___ the doctor who looked ___ him.

6 The doctor sent a bill ___ Savage ___ his visits.

7 He waited ___ several weeks and then sent the bill ___ him again.

8 ___ the end, he came ___ the house and asked ___ his money.

9 I expected gratitude ___ you, as you owe your life ___ me.

10 I am not ungrateful ___ you ___ what you did, so I will give my life ___ you.

11 Tears came ___ the man's eyes and ran ___ his cheeks.

12 A woodcutter was cutting a piece ___ wood ___ his axe ___ a wide river.

13 The axe flew ___ his hand and fell ___ the deep water.

14 The boy rushed ___ the room and shouted ___ an excited voice, 'The house is ___ fire!'

15 There was a big pot ___ water ___ the top ___ the stove.

C

a Copy out these sentences and underline all the **prepositions**.

b Put brackets, (), round each **adjective phrase** and show by an arrow the **noun** it qualifies.

c Draw two lines under this **noun**.

d Round each **adverb phrase** draw a box, ☐ , and show by an arrow the **verb** it modifies.

e Draw three lines under this **verb**.

Examples: The <u>teacher</u> (of the class) explained the lesson.

The boys <u>stood</u> round the room .

1 The driver of the car went fast.
2 She drove down the main road.
3 My mother cut the cake with a knife.
4 The cake was made by my brother.
5 It had been baked in a big oven.
6 It was a cake with pink icing.
7 The boy at the next desk borrowed my pencil.
8 The son of the king is called the Crown Prince.
9 The cat jumped through the window.
10 The lesson finishes at four o'clock.
11 She spoke with a French accent.
12 We played football after the lesson.
13 The sailor with the wooden leg told us a story.
14 The girl with the long hair is Grace Brown.
15 She lives in our street.
16 Grace sang a song at the concert.
17 The men in that country work very hard.
18 The cottage in the woods is very pretty.
19 The sound of the bell was heard all over the house. (2 phrases)
20 After a week or two the doctor sent the bill for his visits. (2 phrases)

D Use these words as **prepositions** in sentences.

Example: under
Answer: The cat is under the table.

1 on	6 from	11 behind	16 along
2 to	7 after	12 through	17 over
3 by	8 for	13 into	18 about
4 of	9 with	14 down	19 between
5 in	10 at	15 near	20 before

Conjunctions

There are now only two more boxes, **conjunctions** and
interjections.

Conjunctions are words that join together words, phrases or
sentences. They are like the links that join railway wagons
together. Here are some examples.

and joins two words

and joins two phrases

but joins two sentences

The woodcutter looked at the gold axe, *but* he refused to take it.

Will you have the gold axe, *or* will you have the silver axe?

Here is a long 'train' joined by conjunctions. It isn't a very good sentence because it has too many conjunctions in it, but it will show you what conjunctions can do.

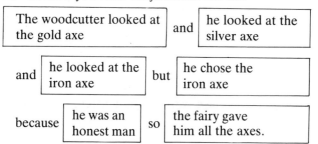

Interjections

There are not many words in this box. They are words (or sometimes phrases, or just noises) that we use to express a sudden feeling, for example, surprise, pleasure, pain, etc.

Here are some: *Hello! Hurrah! Oh! Ah! Good heavens! How pretty! Ouch! Ugh! Wow!*

Note that they usually have an exclamation mark (!) after them.

Exercises

A Join these sentences with the conjunctions *and, but, because, so* or *or*. You will sometimes find it better to leave out one or two words.

Example: We were afraid of them. We ran away.
Answer: We were afraid of them, so we ran away.

1 Grace played the piano. Mary sang a song.
2 Jeremy knocked at the door. His friend opened it.
3 I have a pencil. I have a pen.
4 Tom has a new bicycle. He can't ride it.
5 You must work hard. You won't learn grammar.
6 John walked. Mary came by car.
7 Richard kicked the ball hard. He didn't score.
8 Finish your exercise. You won't be allowed to play football.
9 Mark came to see us. He didn't stay long.
10 We can't play football. We have lost the ball.
11 I lost my book. Richard found it.
12 The fire happened. Ian had left a towel near the stove.
13 The doctor sent a bill to Savage. He hadn't any money. He couldn't pay it. (2 conjunctions)
14 Savage had written a book. Not many copies had been sold. Savage was living in poverty. (2 conjunctions)
15 The boy shook his head. He said, 'That water would be useless. It is hot water.' (2 conjunctions)
16 Newton was a great man. He was very absent-minded.
17 Newton was busy. He told the housekeeper to leave the egg. He told her to go away. (2 conjunctions)
18 She thought he would forget the egg. She returned an hour later. She found Newton standing by the fireplace. (2 conjunctions)
19 Newton was very absent-minded. The housekeeper took an egg to him. She thought he needed food. (2 conjunctions)

B Here are six **interjections** or exclamations and six sentences. Write one of the sentences after the **interjection** that is most suitable. Use each interjection and each

Lesson Twenty

sentence once only. For example, 8 follows 1, so you write:
1 *Hurrah! We've won the match.*

1 Hurrah!	7 I haven't enough money to buy a car like that.
2 Oh!	8 We've won the match.
3 Hello!	9 That hurt me.
4 Ah!	10 I didn't expect to meet you here.
5 How interesting!	11 This is the book I wanted.
6 Ouch!	12 You have been to Italy.